A DAY THAT MADE HISTORY

THE FIRST DAY OF THE SIX DAY WAR

Heather Bleaney and Richard Lawless

Dryad Press   London

Contents

THE EVENTS

THE INVESTIGATION

Acknowledgments

The authors and publishers wish to thank the following for their kind permission to reproduce copyright illustrations: Associated Press, pages 6, 22, 24, 26, 32, 35, 42, 51, 52; The Keystone Collection, pages 9, 11, 16, 21, 30, 31, 37, 45, 53, 57; John Topham Picture Library, frontispiece, page 4. The maps on pages 4, 5, 13, 15, 17, 28, 35, 37, 45, 53 and 57 were drawn by Robert Brien. The pictures were researched by David Pratt.

Cover photographs: Egyptian planes and helicopters destroyed on the ground, June 1967.
Inset: an Israeli pilot poses after a combat mission in his Mirage III fighter.

The "Day that Made History" series was devised by Nathaniel Harris.

© Heather Bleaney and Richard Lawless 1990. First published 1990.
Typeset by Tek-Art Ltd, Kent, and printed and bound by Courier International, Tiptree, Essex
for the publishers, Dryad Press, 4 Fitzhardinge Street, London W1H 0AH

ISBN 0 85219 820 5

THE
EVENTS

The air strike

In spite of the talk of war in the world's press and radio bulletins, on Monday, 5th June, 1967, many Egyptians did not really believe that there was going to be any fighting. Nevertheless, Field Marshal Amer, the Egyptian Commander-in-Chief, set off that morning to start a tour of inspection of his troops in the Sinai Peninsula. By 8.30 a.m., the Ilyushin-14 carrying his party was on its way. At around this time the Egyptians' dawn patrols were due to be returning to base. To ensure Amer's safety, instructions had been given to Egyptian gunners not to open fire on any aircraft over the Sinai.

About 40 Israeli Mirage and Mystère fighter planes had already taken off on their way to Egypt when Marshal Amer's plane appeared on Israeli radar screens, flying in the opposite direction. Deliberately flying very low in order to avoid detection by radar, the first wave of attacking Israeli aircraft struck nine Egyptian airfields almost simultaneously, at approximately 8.45 a.m. Egyptian time. They caught the defending anti-aircraft gunners by surprise. At the moment of the first strike, only four unarmed training aircraft of the Egyptian Air Force were in the air, and they were all shot down.

The nine bases hit were El Arish, Gebel Libni, Bir Gafgafa, Bir Thamada, Abu Sueir, Kabrit, Inchas, Cairo West and Beni Sueif. A tenth, Fayid, was hit a few minutes later. It had still been shrouded in mist when the Israelis came in to the attack, and they had not been able to find it at first. As a second and successive waves of attacking Israeli aircraft appeared in the sky, most of the Egyptian anti-aircraft gunners quickly recovered and fired back.

Eight waves of approximately 40 aircraft bore down on the Egyptian airfields, at about ten-minute intervals. As the first

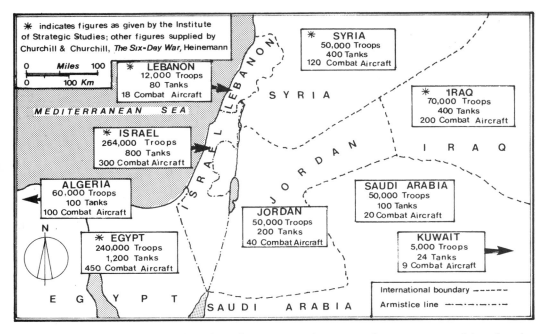

* indicates figures as given by the Institute of Strategic Studies; other figures supplied by Churchill & Churchill, *The Six-Day War*, Heinemann

| 0 | Miles | 100 |
| 0 | 100 Km | |

MEDITERRANEAN SEA

* **LEBANON**
12,000 Troops
80 Tanks
18 Combat Aircraft

* **SYRIA**
50,000 Troops
400 Tanks
120 Combat Aircraft

S Y R I A

* **IRAQ**
70,000 Troops
400 Tanks
200 Combat Aircraft

* **ISRAEL**
264,000 Troops
800 Tanks
300 Combat Aircraft

J O R D A N

I R A Q

ALGERIA
60,000 Troops
100 Tanks
100 Combat Aircraft

SAUDI ARABIA
50,000 Troops
100 Tanks
20 Combat Aircraft

N

* **EGYPT**
240,000 Troops
1,200 Tanks
450 Combat Aircraft

JORDAN
50,000 Troops
200 Tanks
40 Combat Aircraft

KUWAIT
5,000 Troops
24 Tanks
9 Combat Aircraft

E G Y P T

SAUDI ARABIA

International boundary ------
Armistice line —·—·—·—·—

Armed forces in the Middle East on the eve of the war, 1967.

was leaving the target, the second was approaching it, the third already coming up behind, the fourth getting airborne, and the fifth waiting to take off. The Israelis were operating an incredibly fast turn-around time, refuelling, reloading and sending their planes back down the runway in under ten minutes, so that the same plane was back over the same target within an hour. The Egyptians were thus under continuous attack for 80 minutes without respite. From 10.05 to 10.15, there was a ten-minute break, and then another 80 minutes of pounding by successive waves of bombers as before.

Eight Egyptian MiG-21s managed to get airborne and brought down two Israeli Mirages before being themselves shot down. More were destroyed on the runways as they taxied to take off. Twenty Egyptian aircraft (12 MiG-21s and 8 MiG-19s) had been moved south to the airport at Hurghada a few days previously, after the Israelis had deliberately deceived the Egyptians into thinking that they might come in to attack from the Red Sea. These took off after the Israeli assault began and flew north to join the battle. They were either shot down or forced to crashland when they found all the northern runways rendered unusable by Israeli bombing. The Egyptian ground staff worked courageously to repair the runways, but the incessant bombing raids and the use of delayed-action bombs eventually defeated them.

The Egyptians' response to this massive surprise attack was hampered by the fact that their Commander-in-Chief was marooned in the air throughout the first half of the assault and unable to communicate effectively with his forces, while the air force chief, according to one account, was stuck in a Cairo traffic jam, having seen Amer off at the airport. This was an extraordinary piece of good luck for the Israelis. The pilot of Field Marshal Amer's plane sought altitude when he encountered the Israelis coming into attack, in order to stay out of danger, and was only finally able to land at Cairo International civilian airport one-and-a-half hours later. At 11.35 a.m. it was all over. Some 264 combat planes (60% of Egypt's total fighter force) had been destroyed, and the Egyptian Air Force had been effectively eliminated. By this devastating aerial assault, the Israelis had assured themselves

Israeli strikes on Egyptian airfields during the Six Day War. Strikes on northern Syrian bases are not shown.

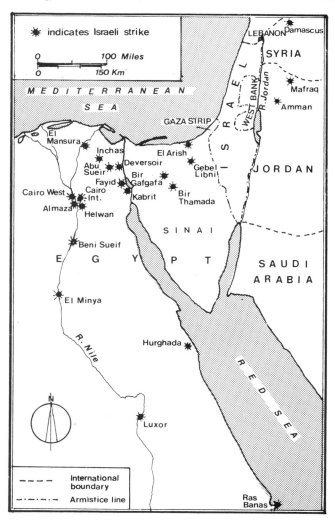

of ultimate victory. They claim to have retained only 12 combat aircraft for home defence and thrown nearly all their forces into this one operation. They had gambled everything on their plan.

The war had only just begun, of course, and the Israeli Air Force, after resting for a couple of hours, and patching up its battered planes, paid several return visits to Egypt later in the day. They resumed attacks, though not quite at the same hectic rate, on the same airfields that had been hit in the morning. They also knocked out the radar stations, which they had ignored earlier. By the end of the day, all 16 Egyptian radar installations in the Sinai had been put out of action.

Altogether, by the end of the first day, the Israeli Air Force had disrupted the 17 major Egyptian airfields and destroyed nearly 300 aircraft, including all 30 of the long-range TU-16

Smoke billows from the Jordanian capital, Amman, during an Israeli air strike on 5 June 1967.

bombers which were caught on the ground at Beni Sueif and Luxor. They claim to have killed about 100 Egyptian pilots and admit to losing only ten of their own aircraft.

The Israelis had good reason to be pleased with the success of their plans which they had worked out and rehearsed over the desert areas of the Negev in southern Israel with the utmost care. Israeli intelligence and target identification were so good that in most cases their pilots ignored the Egyptian dummy aircraft, inflatable mock-ups intended to deceive the enemy and protect the real aircraft from attack. Only at Abu Sueir did they waste time and ammunition on dummies. The Egyptians, both pilots and ground staff, made valiant and courageous attempts to fight back and deal with the invaders, once the assault had begun. Nearly every attacking Israeli aircraft was peppered with shrapnel or bullets from the anti-aircraft gunners. The Egyptians fired a few of their SAM-2 surface-to-air missiles, but these are very slow to pick up speed, and were designed for use against medium- or high-flying planes. They failed to hit their targets, which were flying too low and too fast for them.

During the darkness, the Egyptians managed to repair their runways and installations sufficiently to fly their remaining aircraft to airfields out of the reach of Israeli planes. They also salvaged some of their equipment, including some fighter planes which had only recently arrived and were still in their crates. The surviving Egyptian planes were therefore unable to play much of a role in the following days of the war, although the Egyptians did get some aircraft into action against the Israelis in Sinai later in the week.

The Egyptians had made the task of the attacking aircraft easier, by parking their planes in neat rows on the tarmac as though lined up for inspection. They also concentrated particular types of planes at particular bases, which meant that Israeli planners could expect to catch all the TU-16s, for example, together in the airfields they chose for the initial strike. This practice is not uncommon in other countries, but its consequences in this instance were unfortunate. It is surprising that the long-range TU-16s were not based at airfields out of reach of Israeli aircraft, but still in flying distance of Israeli targets. Mohamed Heikal, Editor-in-Chief of *Al-Ahram* and a close adviser to President Nasser, has argued that Egypt did not believe that Israeli warplanes could have such a massive coverage of all its airfields at the same time. Information from Egyptian intelligence, he maintains, indicated that the range of Israel's fighter planes would not permit them to attack bases in the Nile Delta. Consequently Egyptian planes were parked on the tarmac without protection; this was to be a fatal mistake.

Nasser could not believe the number of planes involved in the attack on his country. His intelligence had accurate information about the size of Israel's air force, and he assumed, as his own air force required, that a turn-around time of approximately one hour on the ground was needed before an aircraft was ready to take off on a second mission. This, together with his experience of a joint Israeli-French-British attack on Egypt in 1956, may have led him to seize on the theory that the British and Americans were participating in the present Israeli attack on Egypt. He stated, in a broadcast to the Egyptian people, that the enemy "was operating an air force three times its normal strength" (Resignation speech, 9th June 1967). In fact, that was not the case, but to the Egyptians, it may have felt like it.

In spite of the magnitude of the disaster which had befallen the Egyptians, Radio Cairo continued to broadcast news of Egyptian victories against the Israelis, and it was nearly midnight before anyone dared to tell President Nasser how much of his air force had actually been destroyed. By then, the Israeli ground forces, in little danger from the Egyptian air force, were already forcing their way into the Sinai Peninsula, knowing that they had only limited time to carry out their plans before the United Nations imposed a cease-fire upon them.

Outside observers concluded, when they learned of the extent of the Egyptian Air Force's losses, that the Israelis had already effectively won the war.

Jordan and Syria and the ground attacks

In the air

The Israeli Air Commander, Brigadier Hod, had reckoned on having a couple of hours in which to deal with the Egyptian Air Force before having to face any threat from those of Jordan and Syria. Israel did not wish to fight on more than one front at once, and hoped that the other Arab countries would stay out of the war. The Israelis deliberately concealed the extent of their success in their strike on Egypt, and allowed the claims of Radio Cairo that Egyptian planes were dealing heavy blows to Israel to go unchallenged. This was intended to add to the enemy's confusion, even at the risk of alarming Israel's civilian population. They also knew that, if Nasser realized that he was facing defeat, he might ask the United Nations to impose a cease-fire before the Israelis had had time to make conquests on the ground. In the event, the Israelis were correct in calculating that it would be some time before Nasser was told the truth by his commanders about the damage inflicted on his air force.

Brigadier Moti Hod, (left) Commander of the Israeli Air force and architect of Israel's success in the air, with Shlomo Har'el, the Naval Commander.

However, the exaggerated claims of Radio Cairo and Israeli silence about its successes had the effect of encouraging both Jordan and Syria to join the war. Nevertheless, neither country got its forces into action until four hours after Israel's first strike on Egypt. The Israeli Air Force did not initiate any hostilities against the Jordanians or the Syrians, but once the Jordanian and Syrian Air Forces attacked targets in Israel, then the IAF hit back with devastating effect. "We were able to deal with Syria and Jordan in twenty-five minutes," Brigadier Hod boasted later.

Some time between 11.00 a.m. and 12 noon on the first morning, Jordanian Hawker Hunters attacked the Netanya airfield in Israel, the airfield at Kfar Sirkin and a few other targets. They destroyed a Noratlas transport aircraft on the ground and returned safely to base. Shortly before noon, Syrian planes attacked Haifa oil refinery and an Israeli airbase near Megiddo, where they shot up some dummy aircraft on the ground. Although the Syrians issued a communiqué stating that Haifa oil refinery was in flames, it had not been touched. Israeli retaliation was swift and powerful.

The Israeli Air force had mostly been resting, refuelling and patching up its aircraft since 10.35 (11.35 Egyptian time), after the end of its first mission against Egypt. Now it turned its attention to these new enemies and at 12.15 launched attacks on both Syria and Jordan. The Israelis destroyed most of the small Syrian Air Force at its bases: the main base at Damascus; the airfields at Marj Rial south of Damascus, "T-4" military airfield on the oil pipeline in the desert, and Seikal. In Jordan, they attacked the two principal air bases at Mafraq and Amman, destroying the small Jordanian Air Force. They also damaged the radar installation at Mount Ajlun in Jordan. Neither the Syrian nor the Jordanian attacks had done very much damage to the Israelis, but those countries paid a heavy price for their acts of aggression.

King Hussein sent his remaining pilots (two had been killed in the Israeli raids) to Iraq, to fly with the Iraqi Air Force, which also had Hawker Hunters. Iraq declared war on Israel, believing from the communiqués issued by the Egyptians that Israel was facing defeat, and hoping to share in the victory. Around 2.00 p.m., an Iraqi squadron launched a bombing raid near the Israeli base at Ramat David. The Israelis were again quick to retaliate: at about 3.00 p.m. they attacked the H-3 military base in northern Iraq and destroyed ten planes on the ground. Most Iraqi bases were out of range of their aircraft.

Egyptian aircraft destroyed on the ground by the Israelis, at an undisclosed airfield.

After dealing with the threats from the east, the Israelis turned their attention back to their most formidable enemy, Egypt, for the rest of the day. As we have seen, they resumed their systematic raids at a more leisurely pace on the airfields which they had hit in the morning, and on some others as well. They also put out of action all 16 Egyptian radar stations in the Sinai, and others in the Delta and Canal regions. Israeli air raids continued on and off after dusk and throughout the night, harassing the Egyptians who were trying to repair runways and salvage aircraft. During the afternoon and evening of the first day, the Israelis practically had the freedom of the skies, only occasionally encountering anti-aircraft fire.

Although the Egyptians and the Syrians still had some planes available, the greater part of both forces had been destroyed.

On the ground: the Egyptian front

At 8.15 a.m. Israeli time (9.15 Egyptian time) on the morning of 5th June, while the Israeli Air Force was hammering Egyptian airfields, the Israeli ground forces started to move towards the Sinai Peninsula in a three-pronged attack. At this stage, they could not know how devastatingly successful the air strike would prove to be, and, even if Israel succeeded in destroying the Egyptian Air Force, the Egyptian Army in Sinai was entrenched in formidable defensive positions.

One Israeli division under the command of Brigadier Tal attacked the Gaza Strip at 9.00 a.m. Israeli time (10.00 a.m. Egyptian time) just south of Khan Yunis and in the vicinity of Rafah. By midnight, after intensive fighting, the main positions held by the Egyptian 7th Infantry Division around Rafah were in Israeli hands. The principal towns of the Gaza Strip – Gaza, Rafah and Khan Yunis – held by the 20th Division of the Palestinian Liberation Army, under the command of the Egyptians and reinforced by regular Egyptian troops, put up fierce resistance and held out.

Israeli troops occupying the town of Gaza, 6 June.

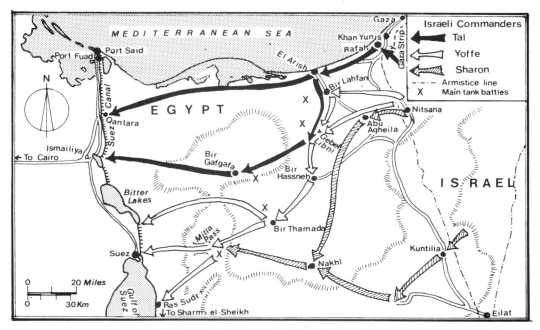

The Israeli advance into Sinai.

The other two Israeli divisions, one commanded by Brigadier Yoffe and the other by Brigadier Sharon, crossed the Israeli-Egyptian border into the Sinai Peninsula at two different places, at the same time as Brigadier Tal attacked the Gaza Strip. They assaulted the Egyptian defensive positions which were initially stoutly defended. By the end of the day, the Israelis were heavily engaged with the Egyptians' first lines of defence, while the bulk of the Egyptian forces in the Sinai were as yet untouched and their morale remained high. All three divisions with which the Israelis had invaded Sinai were exhausted, stuck in the sand, or stranded for lack of fuel, and some were still fighting fierce battles as the first day of the war turned into the second.

On the ground: the Jordanian front

At 8.30 a.m. Israeli time, on the first day, the Israeli Foreign Ministry telephoned General Odd Bull, the United Nations Truce Supervision Organization (UNTSO) chief stationed in Jerusalem, and told him that Egyptian planes had taken off to attack Israel, but had been intercepted (which was untrue). The Israelis asked General Bull to transmit a message to King Hussein of Jordan expressing the hope of the Israeli government that he would not join the war. The Israelis stated that if Jordan stayed out of the hostilities, Israel would not attack, but that if the Jordanians chose to join in, Israel would use against them all the means at its disposal. General Bull states that King Hussein received this message before 10.30 that morning, although King Hussein, in his account, says that he did not get it until after 11.00.

At 08.50 King Hussein's adjutant telephoned him with the news that Radio Cairo "has just announced that the Israelis have launched an assault on Egypt". Ten minutes later, Major-General Riad, the Egyptian commanding the Jordanian Army under the terms of the Arab alliance, received a coded message from Field Marshal Amer in Cairo. The message informed him that Egypt had put out of action 75% of the attacking Israeli planes (which was untrue), and that the Israeli ground attack in Sinai was being successfully contained. Field Marshal Amer ordered Riad to open up a second front against Israel on the Jordanian-Israeli border.

Jordanian artillery opened up a little while later and shelled the outskirts of Tel Aviv and the Israeli military airfield of Ramat David, doing some damage to the installations there and making some craters in the runways. This northern airfield was considered by the Israelis to be of primary importance for their defence of the Galilee, where their relatively small concentrations of troops would be dependent on air support. They did not like the possibility of the airfield's being put out of action, even for a few hours, by Jordanian shelling. This consideration may have been a factor in their decision to launch an attack against Jordan, apparently at a time when the only Jordanian offensive action so far had been long-range artillery fire on the Tel Aviv and Ramat David areas – a sufficient *casus belli*, in fact, if the Israelis were looking for one. Jordanian ground and air offensives did not actually start until after 11.00 a.m. Although the Israeli General Staff had evidently hoped not to fight a war on two fronts at once, they still had carefully prepared plans to face such an eventuality and their troops were ready.

The borders between Israel and its neighbours had been determined by the positions of the Israeli and Arab forces at the end of the war in Palestine in 1948/49. The cease-fire and armistice lines had become de facto frontiers, without regard for geography. The city of Jerusalem had been divided in a rather arbitrary fashion, the Old City (which included the Wailing Wall, the Church of the Holy Sepulchre, and the

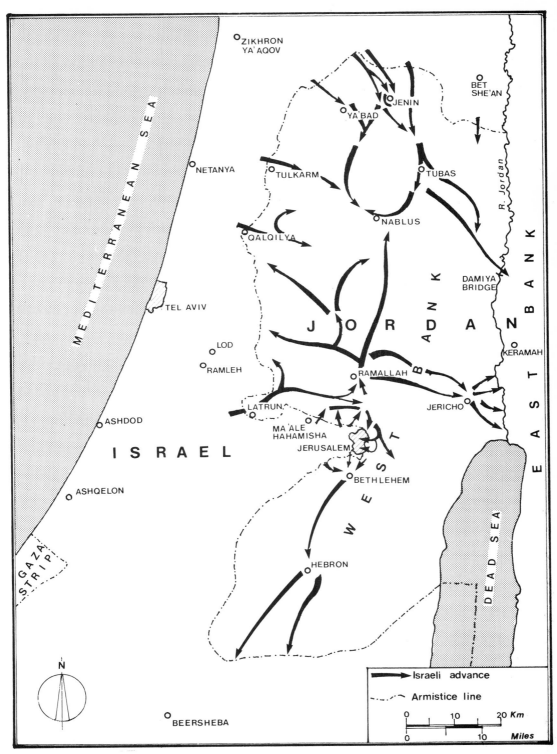

The Israeli advance into the West Bank of Jordan.

Dome of the Rock and al-Aqsa Mosque – places holy to Jews, Christians and Muslims respectively) being in the part under Jordanian control. Mount Scopus, on which were situated the original Hebrew University and Hadassah Hospital (both Jewish foundations), remained as an isolated and technically demilitarized enclave, under Israeli sovereignty, on the Jordanian side. The other demilitarized enclave on the Jordanian side was the area around Government House, which was occupied by the United Nations Truce Supervision Organization.

Although Jordanian guns at various points along the long border with Israel started shelling the outskirts of Tel Aviv and northern Israel some time before 10.00 a.m. on 5th June, the first sustained firing in the Jerusalem area came at about 11.15, when Israeli artillery opened up in response. The Jordanians sent their troops to take over the Government House enclave, where the unarmed United Nations officials offered no resistance. General Uzi Narkiss, the Israeli regional commander, received orders to initiate hostilities in the Jerusalem area shortly before 11.00 a.m. and he immediately put into operation the long-prepared and carefully laid plan for an attack on the Old City, adapting it to the forces now available to him.

Aerial view of Arab or East Jerusalem (showing the Dome of the Rock and Al-Aqsa Mosque) which was captured by Israeli troops from the Jordanians in the Six Day War.

General Narkiss was quickly informed that the Jordanians had taken Government House at about 1.30 p.m., and he prepared to attack it. Shortly before 3.00 p.m., part of an Israeli brigade launched an assault on the newly installed Jordanian positions, which were strategically located on a

The Israeli advance on Jerusalem.

Detailed map of the Old City of Jerusalem.

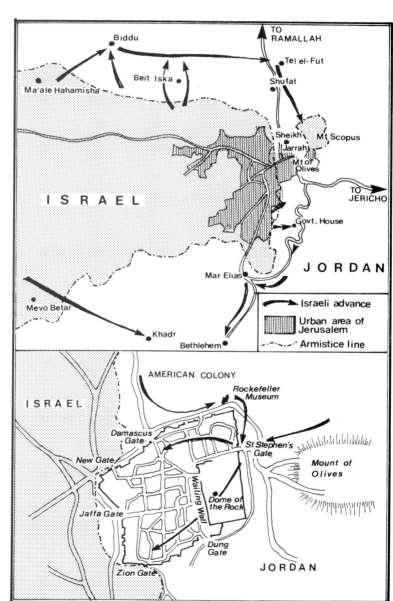

ridge overlooking the Jericho road. By about 4.30, the Jordanian commander realized that he was being surrounded by a combined force of Israeli tanks and infantry, and decided to evacuate the position. The Jordanians carried out an orderly withdrawal towards the northeast, but the battle had been a costly one for them. Meanwhile, the Israelis had been moving their other troops into position for the attack on the Old City. At about 5.00 p.m. they moved across the border north of Jerusalem, against the Jordanian positions there. The Israeli Air Force had wiped out the Jordanian Air Force in the early afternoon and made repeated attacks on Jordanian ground positions in the Jerusalem area.

Brigadier Ata Ali, the Jordanian commander in Jerusalem, lost contact with the West Bank Command Post during the afternoon because Israeli bombing had brought down all the telephone lines, and at 7.30 p.m. the Ramallah radio transmitter fell silent. When Ata Ali managed to regain contact with the command post later in the evening, he learned that the West Bank Command Headquarters, having been bombed out of its command post near Jericho, had withdrawn after sunset, across the river Jordan to the East Bank.

At 8.00 p.m., Brigadier Ata Ali in Jerusalem was informed by radio that he could expect a relief column consisting of one tank battalion of the 60th Armoured Brigade and an infantry battalion from the Qadisiya Brigade, coming from Jericho. But at about 9.00 p.m. the Jordanian defenders in Jerusalem could see flares being dropped, and hear the sound of bombing beyond the Mount of Olives. They were able to guess what was indeed happening – the Israeli Air Force was smashing up the relief column that was supposed to be coming to their aid. Soon after 11.00 p.m., Brigadier Ata Ali was informed by radio that the relief column had been wiped out. Knowing that Israeli reinforcements had come in to surround him, he asked for support, but was told that the other Jordanian troops in the area were expecting to be attacked. However, at about this time, the West Bank Command Headquarters managed to regain contact and informed him that another relief column would be sent from Jericho and would force-march through the hills for the last part of the journey so as to evade Israeli air interception. Ata Ali could expect them to reach the city by early morning.

That was the military situation at the end of the first day.

During the period immediately before the war, the Soviet Union and the United States had reached an agreement that neither would actively intervene in any hostilities in the Middle East if the other stayed out of the fighting. On the morning of 5th June, at 07.59 a.m. New York time (13.59 Israeli time), the "Hot Line" linking the White House and the Kremlin was used for the first time since it had been installed in 1963. The message to US President Johnson from the Soviet government assured the United States that the Soviet Union had no intention of becoming directly involved in the fighting between Israel and Egypt. An hour later, the United States replied reaffirming that America would not participate actively in the conflict. A number of other exchanges took place over the "Hot Line" during 7th and 8th June. It was reported that President Johnson believed that these direct and private exchanges with the Soviet Union had prevented a third world war.

The other five days

As the second day dawned, the war on the ground was still unresolved, although Israeli superiority in the air was making itself felt in the support the air force was lending to its ground forces. The Israeli Air Force was called in by the ground commanders to strafe strongly-held enemy positions in advance of ground assaults, to interdict the movement of enemy troops and supplies, and to disrupt and destroy communications systems. Lack of air cover left the Jordanian and Egyptian armies exposed to attack on the roads and in their fixed positions.

Intense diplomatic activity at the United Nations in New York resulted in the unanimous adoption of a resolution calling for a cease-fire on Tuesday, 6th June. It was not accepted by any of the parties to the war: the Arab delegates argued that Israel should be condemned for aggression, and Israel said that it would not agree to a cease-fire unless the Arab states agreed to accept Israel's statehood and negotiate directly with it. Diplomatic activity at the UN continued throughout the war, led by the USA and the USSR who championed the opposing sides.

In the Air

The Egyptian and Syrian Air Forces still had some planes in service. Between 6th and 9th June, when the war ended, the Israelis had a further 26 encounters with Egyptian aircraft, during which 35 Egyptian planes were lost, and eight encounters with other Arab air forces, in which the Arabs lost four more planes. The Israelis are believed to have lost at least 40 aircraft during the war, of which perhaps a dozen were shot down in dog-fights, the rest falling victim to ground-fire. The Israelis claim that 338 Egyptian, 61 Syrian, 29 Jordanian and one Lebanese aircraft were destroyed during the war, of which 79 were brought down in aerial combat, and the rest destroyed on the ground.

Lebanon had declared war on Israel on the first day, in solidarity with the other Arab states, but had taken no offensive action of any kind and had been left in peace by the Israelis. On the second day, however, two Hawker Hunters from the Lebanese Air Force appeared over northern Israel at about 9.00 a.m. They were intercepted by Israeli aircraft

An Egyptian plane in action against the Israeli army near the Suez Canal during the Six Day War.

and one Lebanese plane was shot down. This was the only clash between the two countries during the war, the pilots having presumably acted on their own initiative. The Lebanese Chief of Staff, General Bustani, was well aware that his small forces were no match for those of Israel.

One other incident in the air war, which has never been satisfactorily explained officially by either side, was the attack on the *USS Liberty*. This specially equipped US Navy vessel was officially designated as an electronics research ship, operating under the command of the US Sixth Fleet but receiving orders directly from the Joint Chiefs-of-Staff in Washington. She was armed with the most complicated systems of radio antennae ever installed on any ship, but carried no offensive weapons. Four machine guns made up her entire defensive capability. When the war broke out, the *Liberty* was at sea in the south-east Mediterranean. On the afternoon of 8th June she was sailing west-northwest, 13½ miles off the Egyptian coast and approximately 60 miles from the nearest Israeli coastline, when Israeli fighter planes and then motor torpedo boats unexpectedly attacked. Thirty-four

American crew members were killed and 164 wounded, and the vessel limped painfully to Malta. The Israelis claimed it was a mistake, and that they had failed to identify the ship as American despite the prominent display of the US flag. However, the attack continued even after the ship had made itself known to the attackers. The Israelis expressed regret, but never apologized or admitted culpability. The suspicion remains that the Israelis knew the ship to be American from the start, and attacked it because they feared that the vessel's sophisticated intelligence-gathering equipment would harm Israel by spying on their war plans. The US government chose to play down the incident.

The USS Liberty lying crippled in Athens on 9 June 1967. A gaping hole from an Israeli torpedo shows near the waterline.

On the ground: the Jordanian front

On the Jordanian front, the Israelis were advancing into the West Bank and closing in on Jerusalem by the end of the first day. The Jordanians knew that they had no air cover for their troops and they were worried about their situation. The Iraqis had sent one brigade of troops to their aid, but it had been caught by the Israeli Air Force and in fact never went into action against the Israelis. The Syrians offered no help and, on the evening of the first day, had sent a signal that they could not do so because they had no air cover. Nevertheless, the Jordanians fought stubbornly and hard and the outcome was by no means certain.

Early in the small hours of the second day, the Israelis began their assault on the Old City of Jerusalem, and by the end of the day it had become clear to Brigadier Ata Ali that he would be unable to hold the Jordanian positions. He saw that it made more military sense to withdraw his forces intact and not try to defend the city to the bitter end. Accordingly, during the darkness of the following night, the Jordanian defenders made an organized and undetected withdrawal. At 10.30 a.m. on the third day, Wednesday, 7th June, the Arab Governor of East Jerusalem, accompanied by the religious head, met the Israeli Brigade Commander and gave him an undertaking that there would be no more resistance. He explained that the last Jordanian troops had already left. Opposition ceased. Israeli fortunes on the Jordanian front thus changed dramatically on the third day, from uncertainty at dawn to triumph by nightfall. Practically the whole of the West Bank was in Israeli hands, and the Jordanian Army was frantically trying to salvage its men and equipment and retreat across the river Jordan to protect the East Bank.

On Wednesday, 7th June, the United Nations unanimously adopted a second resolution, this time demanding that governments concerned in the fighting "cease fire and all military activities on 7 June 1967 at 2000 hours GMT (2200 Israel time)". At 7.15 p.m. Israeli time, the UN Secretary General, U Thant, announced that the Jordanian government had accepted the cease-fire. The Israeli Foreign Minister, Abba Eban, replied that, while Israel welcomed the cease-fire resolution, Egypt, Iraq and Syria had not accepted it, and Jordan's acceptance of it was of doubtful value because Jordanian forces were under Egyptian command. On Thursday, 8th June, after Egypt had accepted the cease-fire

unconditionally at 9.35 p.m. Israeli time (10.35 p.m. Egyptian time), the Soviet delegate to the UN accused Israel of ignoring the cease-fire and continuing to take by force new territories belonging to Egypt and Jordan. The Israeli delegate replied that the cease-fire with Jordan had become effective, which by Thursday afternoon was indeed the case. The Israelis now controlled all the West Bank of Hussein's kingdom, and the river Jordan formed the new cease-fire line between Israel and Jordan.

On the ground: the Egyptian front

While the Israelis had made inroads into the Sinai Peninsula and the Gaza Strip by the end of the first day, the principal Egyptian lines of defence remained intact, their men were putting up stubborn resistance and morale was fairly high. However, during the second day the Israeli push continued, several ground battles were lost, and the Israeli Air Force appeared in numbers to carry out air strikes and interdiction tasks deep into the Sinai Peninsula, while there was an almost complete absence of Egyptian planes overhead. The Egyptians could take some encouragement from the shooting down of two or three Israeli planes, but the outlook for the troops in Sinai was becoming bleaker.

At about noon on the second day, General Murtagi, the commander of the Egyptian land forces in Sinai, realized, perhaps for the first time, that the official Egyptian radio communiqués were false and that the Egyptian Air Force had been practically destroyed. He had also by this time lost communication with a large part of his command, and so was unable to manoeuvre his troops in a battle whose outcome was still uncertain. He ordered his men to withdraw to the main defensive line along the Central Ridge, and while some units evidently received the message, others were cut off and unsure whether to stand and fight or to retreat. By the end of the second day, there was considerable confusion within the Egyptian forces in the Sinai and this spread rapidly, to verge almost on panic at headquarters.

It seems that early on the morning of 6th June, the second day of the war, as news of the Israeli advances in the Sinai and Gaza Strip came into the Egyptian HQ, Field Marshal Amer decided to withdraw from the Sinai Peninsula and concentrate all Egyptian forces behind the Suez Canal. Apparently he did not consult President Nasser about this.

◁ *Moshe Dayan (right), Israeli Minister of Defence, with Brigadier Uzi Narkiss (Israeli Commander on the Jordanian Front) at the Wailing Wall after the capture of the Old City of Jerusalem, 7 June 1967.*

Brigadier-General Ariel Sharon (left) and Brigadier-General Avraham Yoffe (right), Israeli Commanders on the Egyptian Front with Menachem Begin, later Prime Minister of Israel, 13 June 1967.

Nor did he consult his staff, who had contingency plans to deal with just such an Israeli attack and were prepared to implement them. Many of the division commanders in the Sinai were, like Amer himself, political appointees rather than professional soldiers, and seem to have been more concerned to save their own skins than to fight the enemy. Pausing only long enough to pass on the order to withdraw, without further explanation or instructions, many of the senior commanders ordered their cars to head west to safety, abandoning their men.

The Egyptian General Staff at Headquarters, who were beginning to recover from the first shock of the Israeli attack, received another blow when they learned that Amer had sent withdrawal orders directly to the commanders in the Sinai. They had been counting on implementing the original plan of mounting a big counter-offensive against the Israelis as they reached the central Sinai, and they were completely unprepared for Amer's decision to withdraw. Three senior staff officers demanded to see him immediately. Their chief had cut himself off from all direct contact with his staff since the previous night, but after a brief delay, they managed to get in to see him. They convinced Amer that his order could only end in the loss of all the Sinai Peninsula, and he authorized them to send out messages to stop the withdrawal. Unfortunately, except for units already out of touch with their headquarters, elements of the four front-line divisions were already retreating, and some of those whose retreat was cut off by the advancing Israelis were disintegrating. The disaster feared by the Egyptian generals was already becoming a fact.

By late on Tuesday, 6th June, it was clear to the Israeli commanders in the Sinai that a full-scale Egyptian withdrawal was taking place. The Egyptians had changed from stubborn defence to delaying tactics, and Israeli air reconnaissance was reporting massive Egyptian movements to the west. The Israelis had been given the mission of destroying the Egyptian Army in the Sinai, but it was becoming clear that the major part of that army might escape from them back across the Suez Canal. The Israelis' political objectives also required that they make the maximum possible military gains on the ground. Accordingly, they not only pursued the retreating Egyptian army, but deliberately raced their own forces towards the Suez Canal.

On the morning of 7th June, the first Israeli units reached the eastern bank of the Suez Canal, but were promptly ordered by the Minister of Defence, Moshe Dayan, to withdraw a few miles. This may have been because he did not want international pressure for a cease-fire to be increased at a time when the Israeli forces were far from having secured their major objectives; but in any case he did not have sufficient military strength in the area to control all the territory to the east of the canal.

The second cease-fire resolution adopted by the UN Security Council had been formally accepted only by Jordan on 7th June at 7.15 p.m. Israeli time. The Israelis had welcomed the cease-fire called for 10.00 p.m. Israeli time, but avoided formally accepting it, indicating that Egypt, Iraq and Syria had not yet done so. The Israeli advance into Sinai continued and on the next day, Thursday, 8th June, the other Israeli divisions also broke through to the canal, harassing and chasing the retreating Egyptian forces. By about midday on 8th June, the entire Sinai Peninsula, except for the marshlands east of Port Fuad, was under Israeli control.

On the afternoon of 8th June in New York, the Security Council reassembled because the deadline for the cease-fire had passed without an end to the fighting. The USA said that, apart from Jordan, the Arab government had not accepted the cease-fire, while the USSR condemned Israel for

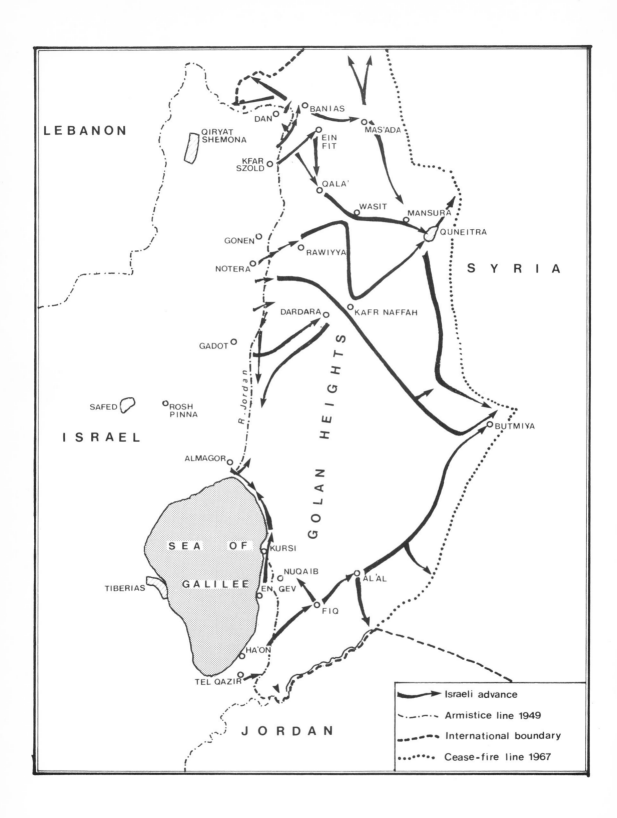

LEBANON

QIRYAT
SHEMONA

DAN ○
○ BANIAS

EIN
FIT
○ MAS'ADA

KFAR
SZOLD ○

QALA' ○

WASIT
○
MANSURA
○
○ QUNEITRA

GONEN ○

RAWIYYA ○
NOTERA ○

S Y R I A

DARDARA ○

KAFR NAFFAH ○

GADOT ○

R. Jordan

G O L A N   H E I G H T S

SAFED
○ ROSH
PINNA

I S R A E L

BUTMIYA ○

ALMAGOR ○

S E A   O F

KURSI ○

NUQAIB
○
AL 'AL ○

G A L I L E E

TIBERIAS

EN GEV ○

FIQ ○

HA'ON ○

TEL QAZIR ○

J O R D A N

	Israeli advance
—·—·—	Armistice line 1949
– – –	International boundary
··········	Cease-fire line 1967

28

aggression and for violating two cease-fire resolutions already passed. At about 3.30 p.m. in New York (9.30 p.m. Israeli time,
10.30 p.m. Egyptian time), the Security Council was informed that Egypt had "decided to accept the cease-fire call . . . on the condition that the other party ceases fire". The Israeli delegate replied only that Israel would study the draft resolution. A cease-fire on the Egyptian front did not take hold until the early hours of Friday morning, Egyptian time (9.35 p.m. on Thursday, 8th June, in New York), when Egypt accepted an unconditional cease-fire and the Israelis were in control of nearly all the Sinai Peninsula.

On the ground: the Syrian front

There was not very much ground activity on the Syrian front during the first four days of the war. The Syrians had kept up constant heavy shelling of the Israeli forces below the Golan Heights, to which the Israelis replied with artillery fire and frequent air strikes on Syrian positions. On 6th June, the second day, three Syrian reconnaissance patrols moved into Israeli territory in the extreme north of Israel, and were repulsed. With the destruction of their air force, the Syrians had given up any idea of an offensive into northern Galilee by the evening of the 6th, and all movements of men and material were subject to attack by the Israeli Air Force. They therefore contented themselves with shelling Israeli Army concentrations and fortified kibbutzim (agricultural settlements that formed the spearhead of Zionist colonization) near the frontier, but made no further attempt to invade Israeli territory. The Israelis, on the other hand, were keen to take the offensive in order to capture the Golan Heights and inflict heavy punishment on the Syrians. For years, the Syrian Army, in response to Israeli provocations, had shelled kibbutzim inside Israel from their gun emplacements on the Golan Heights, which overlooked Israeli towns and villages in the plains below. The Heights were therefore an important strategic objective for the Israeli military.

At 3.20 a.m. on Friday, 9th June, shortly after Egypt had accepted a cease-fire, Syria, which had no wish to fight the Israelis alone, announced that it, too, agreed to it. The victorious Israelis, however, were reluctant to halt the fighting before they had achieved all their military objectives. The Israeli Minister of Defence, Moshe Dayan, had previously strongly opposed an attack on Syria, but he

◁ *The Israeli advance into Syria.*

29

Levi Eshkol, Israeli Prime Minister (centre), visits Israeli troops on the Syrian Front before the ceasefire which finally became effective on 11 June 1967.

changed his mind when he heard that both Syria and Egypt had accepted the cease-fire, and that Israeli intelligence was reporting that the Syrian town of Quneitra was empty and that the Syrian front was beginning to collapse. At 7.00 a.m., some 3½ hours after Syria had accepted the cease-fire, he gave the order to attack.

At 11.30 a.m. Israeli troops, with massive air support, assaulted the Syrian fortified positions on the Golan Heights, which had already been pounded by prolonged artillery bombardment. After stiffly resisting at first, the Syrian defenders began to give way, and, once the Israelis had broken through the front line, the Syrian defence everywhere started to crumble. At noon, the Syrian government protested strongly to the UN Security Council about Israel's violation of the cease-fire, and ordered its forces to withdraw from the line of the Golan Heights to defensive positions around Damascus, the capital. In the UN, Israel blamed Syria for continued shelling after the start of the cease-fire, and so accusations were traded in the Security Council while conflicting reports of the fighting were presented.

The collapsing morale of Syria's troops was further undermined by Damascus Radio's false report that Quneitra had fallen, before Israeli troops had even reached it. By making this announcement, the Syrian government had hoped to spur the Security Council into adopting a cease-fire resolution and stopping the Israeli advance. Once the Israelis had captured the Golan Heights, the Syrians feared that they would drive swiftly across the plains and take Damascus not far away. Syria's political ally, the USSR, exerted diplomatic pressure in the Security Council on the Americans and on the Israelis to prevent such an eventuality. The Americans, while not unwilling to see Israel benefit from the war, began to worry about the extent of Israeli ambitions, and insisted that Israel must accept a cease-fire, as its aggressive behaviour was becoming difficult for the Americans to defend at the UN.

An Israeli soldier stands guard over Egyptian prisoners of war captured in Sinai during the Six Day War.

Lt General Yitzhak Rabin, the Israeli Chief-of Staff, was reluctant to halt his forces until Israel had captured Quneitra and established a defensible line east of the Golan Heights. He therefore instructed Abba Eban, the Foreign Minister, to stall for time at the UN, until the Israeli troops were sure of obtaining their objectives. When the Security Council finally approved a resolution calling for a cease-fire effective from

Israeli tanks in action during fierce fighting on the border with Syria on 10 June 1967.

6.30 p.m. Israeli time on Saturday, 10th June, Israeli troops were more or less ready to comply. The Syrians accused the Israelis of further military activity and troop movements after the cease-fire was due to start, but on Sunday, 11th June, when UN observers moved into place, all was quiet on the last war front.

At sea

The Israeli Navy was by far the least strong of the three services. Its major war goal was to weaken the Egyptian naval presence in the Mediterranean as much as possible, in order to diminish the threat to the Israeli population centres on the coast. By skilful use of deception, the Israelis managed to persuade the Egyptians that an Israeli naval attack on Sharm el-Sheikh was imminent. This Egyptian military post controlled the approaches to Eilat, Israel's only non-Mediterranean port. In the event of war, it would be an obvious target for Israeli attack, to prevent the Egyptians cutting Israel's alternative supply route to Eilat. On the outbreak of hostilities, 30% of the Egyptian fleet was in the Red Sea, where it could contribute little to the Egyptian war effort. When President Nasser blocked the Suez Canal at the end of the war by sinking ships in it, his own vessels were cut off from the Mediterranean, and they finally docked at the Yemeni port of Hodeida in the Red Sea.

The Egyptian Navy was not really alerted to the possibility of war, even as late as early June. President Nasser, not intending to let the crisis get out of hand and degenerate into war, had not called for more than the usual degree of alertness on the part of the Navy. When war suddenly broke out, it was quite unready for anything other than general coastal defence and local security. By the time the Egyptian Navy was starting to move into its planned blockading stations, the end of the war halted further deployment.

There was little substantial naval activity by either side during the war. Both the Israelis and the Egyptians carried out one or two missions with little success. They did not have any effect on the course of the war.

THE INVESTIGATION

Whose fault was it?

Israel had always known that Egypt was the most powerful of the hostile Arab countries on its borders. Israeli military commanders had therefore spent years planning for the possibility of a war with Egypt. Brigadier Hod said at a press conference given in Tel Aviv in June 1967: "For 16 years we lived with the plan, we slept with the plan, we ate with the plan. Constantly we perfected it." The reasons for the hostility between Israel and its neighbours are rooted in the manner of Israel's birth as a state.

Zionism, Britain and Palestine

During the First World War, Britain made promises to both the Arabs and the Jews. In 1915, Britain agreed to recognize and support an independent Arab state in return for their aid in the war against the Turks. This Arab state would include all the Arab lands from present-day Saudi Arabia north to present-day Lebanon and Syria, including Palestine, Syria and most of Iraq. Two years later, in 1917, the British Foreign Secretary, Balfour, pledged Britain's support for the establishment of a Jewish "national home" in Palestine. When the war ended, the defeated Ottoman (Turkish) Empire was partitioned by the victorious Allies. Britain assumed responsibility for Palestine under a League of Nations mandate. The terms under which the Mandate of Palestine was granted to Britain reaffirmed the Balfour Declaration. From the outset, the British administration in the "twice promised" land of Palestine was faced with the impossible task of trying to reconcile two opposing nationalisms – one Jewish, under the name Zionism, and the other Arab. The Zionists wished to build a Jewish state in Palestine to which Jews in the diaspora would return and live among their own people. Then they would no longer suffer from the weakness of being a religious minority in other states. However, Jewish immigration began to decline after initial enthusiasm in the early years of the mandate. The Arab population of Palestine was alarmed by Zionist propaganda and activities and feared that the newcomers were going to take over their land.

After the outbreak of the Second World War, the horrifying Nazi policy of exterminating Jews in Europe reached ever more frightening proportions and the British authorities were faced with a rising tide of Jewish immigration into Palestine. Exhausted by war with Germany, Britain found its mandate over Palestine unworkable, and the obligations undertaken to the two communities irreconcilable. In desperation, on 2nd April, 1947, Britain referred its mandate over Palestine back to the League of Nations' successor, the United Nations.

The United Nations Organization, with its headquarters in New York, decided in November 1947 that Palestine should be partitioned into two parts, an Arab state and a Jewish state, and that the city of Jerusalem should have a special

The UN plan for the partition of Palestine, 1947.

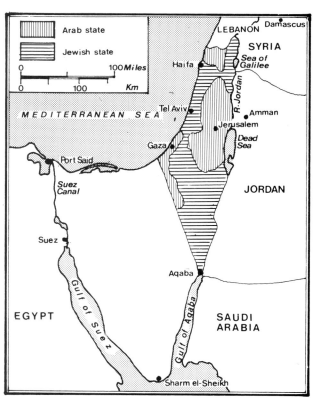

David Ben Gurion proclaims the independence of the State of Israel in Tel Aviv on 14 May 1948.

international regime, because of its religious significance to Christians, Jews and Muslims. At that time, the Jews made up only a third of the population in Palestine and owned a mere 6% of the land. Nevertheless, 55% of Palestine was allotted to the proposed Jewish state, while the Arabs, who were the great majority of the people, were awarded less than half of their homeland for an Arab state. Even in the proposed Jewish state, there were more Arabs than Jews. Naturally, the Arab population could not accept such a plan, which required them to surrender a large part of their own country, and so they rejected it out of hand. The Jewish Agency, on the other hand, decided to accept the partition plan, although it is clear that from the outset the Zionists were not prepared to accept the proposed partition boundaries. For them, the partition plan was only the first step to achieving their real demands.

The birth of Israel

On 15th May 1948, the British government's mandate over Palestine came to an end. The Jews in Palestine proclaimed the State of Israel, but never defined the borders of the new state. Even before 15th May, they had already carried out military operations to drive the Arabs out of the areas of Palestine allotted to the Jewish state under the UN partition plan, and out of some of the areas allotted to the Arab state as well. The Palestinian Arabs had very few weapons, as the British had never allowed them to re-arm themselves after brutally suppressing their rebellion during 1936-38. The Jews, by contrast, were both well-armed and very well-organized. Once the British left, as their commander was well aware, the Jewish units would be strong enough to take the whole of Palestine by force and, if necessary, to defeat the ill-equipped armies of the surrounding Arab states too. On 15th May, the neighbouring Arab countries, in response to inflamed public opinion demanding that they do something to prevent the dispossession of the Palestinians who were already fleeing from their country, sent their armies in to try to salvage for the Palestinian Arabs the areas of their country that had been allotted to them under the UN plan. They did not succeed.

The State of Israel after the 1948 war.

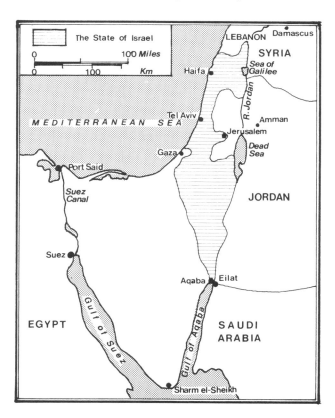

**The Palestinians
become refugees**

In the war that followed, and finally ended with armistice agreements in 1949, the new State of Israel increased its territory considerably. The Arab state which the UN partition plan had intended to be established disappeared from the map; the area in the south round Gaza city, which the Egyptian army had held, was subsequently ruled by an Egyptian administration on a temporary basis; the eastern half of Palestine, and the eastern part of Jerusalem (including the Old City) were held by the Jordanian Army. In 1950, this area was annexed to the Kingdom of Jordan and became commonly known as the West Bank (of the river Jordan).

As a result of this war, some 800,000 Palestinian Arabs were rendered homeless refugees, living outside the borders of the new state of Israel, while those who remained within it were placed under military rule. The Palestinians who had fled hoped that they would be able to return to their homes and villages once the fighting had ended. The United Nations General Assembly had resolved on 11th December, 1948, that those refugees wishing to return to their homes should be permitted to do so and that compensation should be paid to those who did not wish to return. Yet Israel consistently refused to implement the resolution. Indeed, it proceeded to demolish some 386 Arab villages so that there could be no going back. The homes and villages from which Palestinians had fled became quickly no more than a memory. Very soon, Arab land was being occupied and farmed by Jews. Some of the refugees, now deprived of their livelihood, could actually see their own lands being cultivated by Israelis on the other side of the new border. This sharpened their sense of loss and frustration.

**The Arab revolutions
and Nasser's rise to
power**

In the years following the defeats suffered by the Arab armies in Palestine in 1948-49, the Arab countries experienced considerable political upheaval. Popular feelings were inflamed by the loss of Palestine, the plight of the refugees and the miserable showing of the Arab armies which their leaders had led them to believe would be triumphant and victorious. Most of these countries had themselves only recently acquired their independence from colonial powers, and their regimes were faced with profound domestic problems. The creation of the state of Israel, and the closing of its borders after the war which followed, cut off traditional markets, supplies and trading routes in the region and caused severe economic problems for Jordan and Syria.

Syria suffered a number of military coups in rapid

---

succession, and remained rather unstable throughout the 1950s and 1960s. In Jordan, King Abdullah was assassinated by a Palestinian in 1951 and was eventually succeeded by his grandson, King Hussein. In Egypt, King Farouk was deposed and sent into exile by the Free Officers who staged a successful coup in 1952. In 1954, Gamal Abdul Nasser became President of Egypt. He was a great champion of Arab nationalism and soon became the acknowledged leader of the Arab world – acknowledged by the masses, that is, for there were other Arab leaders who would also have liked to be able to claim that position for themselves. In spite of much talk about the importance of Arab unity, there was a good deal of distrust and rivalry between the different Arab regimes. The League of Arab States (often called simply the "Arab League") had been formed in 1945 to strengthen the Arab countries by co-operating economically and politically, but the Arab rulers did not find it easy to work together.

Nasser's early encounters with the Israelis

When Nasser came to power, his priorities were to terminate the British military presence in Egypt and to end foreign control over Egypt's economic and commercial affairs – principally foreign management of the Suez Canal. Under the terms of the treaty of 1936, Egypt had become formally independent, but Britain retained the right to station troops

The Suez Canal.

in the Canal Zone for 20 years. Such foreign presence offended the Egyptians' national pride and prevented them from gaining true independence and control over their own affairs. Nasser also wished to see Egypt develop socially and economically and its people raised out of their crushing poverty.

In common with the rest of the Arab world, President Nasser regarded the dispossession of the Palestinians as an injustice. No solution to the Arab-Israeli conflict would be acceptable to the Arabs unless it enabled the Palestinians to return to their country. However, he was well aware of Israel's strength and diplomatic support abroad. He did not think that the Arabs were in a position to force a satisfactory solution, and he did not wish to provoke a war with Israel which the Arabs would certainly lose, at least until their military strength had been built up. At the same time, he tried to keep open the option of either a military or a political solution.

To this end, he entered into secret talks with the Israelis while Moshe Sharett was Prime Minister in 1954. However, David Ben-Gurion and others in the Israeli establishment disagreed with the idea of trying to negotiate with the Egyptians, and when Ben-Gurion became Prime Minister again, shortly afterwards, he returned to a more interventionist foreign policy with regard to Israel's Arab neighbours. In February 1955, an unprovoked attack by the Israelis on Gaza left 39 Egyptian soldiers dead. Nasser later described this raid as a turning point. He could no longer ignore the demands of his army and the Palestinian refugees for arms, nor Egyptian public opinion demanding that something be done. An arms race followed, fuelling fears on either side, and raids across the border by Palestinian fedayeen (guerrilla fighters) drew fierce Israeli reprisal raids.

The Suez Crisis This led directly to war in 1956. A massive arms deal between Egypt and Czechoslovakia in 1955 alarmed Israel, while Nasser's nationalization of the Suez Canal Company enraged Britain and France. In response, Israel, Britain and France came to a secret agreement for a co-ordinated attack on Egypt, aimed at destroying its charismatic leader. On 29th October, 1956, Israel invaded Sinai and two days later, as previously arranged, Britain and France mounted air attacks on Egypt and landed troops at Port Said. World opinion was outraged by this blatant aggression. Under strong pressure from America, whose president, Eisenhower, had not been informed of the plans for the joint attack, the British and French troops were evacuated and the Israelis forced to give up Sinai.

After this experience, President Nasser became more and more convinced that Israel was a danger to the Arab states. He saw Israel as a tool of Western imperialism in the area, and as part of a conspiracy aimed at destroying him.

The road to war in 1967

In 1967, Nasser's attempt to pursue a precarious policy of co-existence-without-peace and hostility-without-war led him for a second time into a crisis which he could not control. Israel had continually flouted UN resolutions and hindered UN peace-keeping efforts. It had refused to have UN troops stationed on its side of the border since 1957, and had six times been condemned by the Security Council for its military reprisal attacks on neighbouring Arab countries. Nasser wished to reassure the other Arab nations and his own people that Israel could not do as it pleased with impunity, but at the same time he was not ready for all-out war. As late as January 1967, Nasser did not think that the conflict with Israel was about to flare up, and even when tension started to rise, he did not intend to let it turn into full-scale war. Nasser does not seem to have taken into account the effect his threatening broadcasts and troop movements would have on the Israelis, or what their likely response would be. The Syrian government played a major role in heightening tensions (see below). But finally it was the action of an anxious Jordanian government, in joining a military alliance with Egypt and Syria, which stung the Israelis into action.

Neither Egypt nor Israel intended to go to war in 1967, but they became locked into an upward spiral of belligerent statements and threatening gestures. Both sides contributed to the series of escalations which led to the outbreak of hostilities, and it would be difficult to say that one was more responsible than the other. The Israeli generals were confident that if it came to war, Israel would be able to win, and the Israeli government understood that the Americans would not oppose them as they had done in 1956. The Soviet Union, which supported President Nasser, was not expected to intervene directly.

The propaganda war

In February 1966, Syria suffered yet another coup (the 17th in 21 years), and the new government was militantly anti-Zionist. It established close relations with the Soviet Union, from which it began to receive arms supplies, and it

President Nasser of Egypt (centre) with Egyptian Commander in Chief Abdel-Hakim Amer (right) signs a military alliance with Iraq on 4 June 1967, one day before the outbreak of war. On the left the Deputy Premier of Iraq Taher Yahya.

encouraged the Palestinian nationalist guerrilla groups to mount raids into Israeli territory. It also became more friendly towards Egypt, and in November 1966 the two countries established a defence agreement. All this was viewed by the Israelis with some alarm. They intensified their heavy reprisal raids on Syria and Jordan, which served as bases for the Palestinian guerrilla fighters infiltrating into Israel. These reprisal raids were mounted partly as a matter of government policy, in the hope that they would deter the infiltrators, and partly to mollify Israeli public opinion. A pattern similar to the build-up to the Suez War in 1956 was in danger of becoming established.

After some severe clashes on the Syrian and Jordanian borders, both the Syrian and Jordanian governments accused Nasser of failing to support them in the confrontation with Israel, in spite of his claims to be the leader of a "United Arab Nation". By May 1967, Moscow, Cairo and Damascus were all genuinely alarmed by Israeli threats of action against Syria. On 11th May, the Israeli representative at the United Nations stated that as long as the Syrian government continued with its "unrealistic and aggressive policy . . . the Government of Israel . . . regards itself as fully entitled to act in self-defence as circumstances warrant". A few days later, the Israeli Minister of Labour, Y. Allon, told a reporter that Syria "could be the victim of crushing assaults" if it attempted a "popular war" against Israel. Whether or not Israel meant these and other public statements on the radio and in the press to be no more than a warning, they caused the Syrians to ask Nasser to pledge his solidarity and support for them. President Nasser therefore decided that he must do something to restore his crumbling prestige in the Arab world.

No way back   Three particular events led to the outbreak of war: the withdrawal of the United Nations Emergency Force from the Egyptian-Israeli border; the blockage of the Straits of Tiran to Israeli shipping (this was regarded by the Israelis as a belligerent act even if Nasser did not intend to enforce it); and the reconciliation of President Nasser with King Hussein of Jordan.

The United Nations Emergency Force (UNEF)   UNEF was created in 1956, after the Israelis had withdrawn from the Sinai Peninsula, in order to prevent incidents between Egypt and Israel. The force was stationed on Egyptian territory, because the Israelis never agreed to have it on their side of the border. On 16th May, 1967, the commander of the UNEF force in the Sinai, Major General Rikhye, received a letter from General Mohamad Fawzi, the Egyptian Chief of Staff, demanding the withdrawal of all UN forces from the border with Israel. He transmitted the request to the UN Secretary General, U Thant, who told the Egyptians that only he himself could authorize the withdrawal of UN troops, and that if Egypt submitted this request to him, he would also order the withdrawal of all other UNEF troops stationed in Gaza and the rest of the Sinai Peninsula.

It seems that President Nasser had not meant to precipitate this crisis, but had miscalculated. He had probably expected that a meeting of the Security Council would have to be called and that it would then decide that the forces should stay in position. In that case, Nasser would have safely made a show of demanding UNEF's withdrawal, without having to face the consequences of its being carried out. However, the Secretary General's reply indicated that, if the Egyptian government demanded it, he could order the withdrawal of UNEF without consulting the Security Council. Nasser evidently felt that, having once made the demand, he could not now back down, and so, after delaying for a couple of days, he submitted an official demand to the Secretary General for the withdrawal of the UN troops. Since the Israeli government had only that morning reiterated its refusal to have UN troops stationed on its side of the border, U Thant issued the order for UNEF's withdrawal.

The Israeli government viewed this development as an indication that Egypt might attack.

The blockade of the Straits of Tiran

Meanwhile, on 15th May, Egyptian troops had started moving into new positions in the Sinai, mostly into the corner nearest to Israel, around Rafah and El Arish, and by 22nd May the number of troops in the Sinai had nearly doubled. On that day President Nasser announced his intention to close the Straits of Tiran to Israeli shipping. The Straits of Tiran control access to the Gulf of Aqaba and the Israeli port of Eilat. Israel had made it clear publicly that such a move would be considered an act of war.

Once again Nasser miscalculated. It seems that he expected the Israelis to test the seriousness of his intentions by trying to send some ships through the Strait. He would then be able to prove to the Israelis that he did not really mean to enforce a physical blockade and thus precipitate war. He merely wanted to reaffirm a state of existing hostility, to impress his Arab neighbours. However, the Israelis took his announcement at face value. They did not try to send a ship through the Straits to see if Nasser would stop them. They regarded the declaration of the blockade as "a clear act of war, which surely justified military counteraction", as Moshe Dayan explained in his memoirs. They resolved to strike Egypt before they themselves were attacked, as they were convinced that Arab states, and Nasser in particular, were bent on war, and hostile broadcasts and public statements in the Arab capitals of Cairo, Damascus and Baghdad were threatening Israel with destruction.

The reconciliation of Nasser and Hussein

Not only were the Israelis worried by the rising tide of belligerent threats; they were genuinely alarmed by the sudden reconciliation between King Hussein of Jordan and President Nasser. On 30th May King Hussein flew to Cairo, accompanied by his Prime Minister, Chief-of-Staff and Commander of the Air Force, and concluded with Nasser a mutual defence pact. This brought Jordan into the joint military alliance with Egypt and Syria, under the nominal overall command of the Egyptians. On the same day, the

King Hussein of Jordan (front) visits Jordanian army positions in frontier areas shortly before the outbreak of war on 5 June 1967.

Egyptians appointed an Egyptian General, Abdul Moneim Riad, a respected senior officer in the Egyptian Army, as the joint commander of Arab forces on the Jordanian front.

On 2nd June, General Riad arrived with a small staff to take over his new command, and the next day three battalions of Egyptian commandos were flown to Amman. To the Israelis, now surrounded by a united Arab military alliance, those actions could only be interpreted as serious preparations for war, although it is very clear in retrospect that Nasser did not in fact have any intention of precipitating war against Israel. He was apparently well aware that his army was woefully unprepared for such a war, and he remembered that in 1960, in somewhat similar circumstances, he had increased the garrison in the Sinai and threatened a war against Israel and nothing had happened. He was delighted that, as a result of his public statements and political activity, he had restored his prestige in the Arab world and he appeared also to have scored a political victory over Israel, which now seemed to be backing down from a confrontation with him.

Nasser's misjudgement It seems incredible that Nasser should not have recognized that the situation was not the same as it had been in 1960, that he was not dealing with the same leaders in Israel, and that the Israelis could not be expected to sit back and wait to see if he was going to attack them. Moreover, they had their own public opinion to consider, and the Prime Minister, Levi Eshkol, was not a leader of such towering strength and prestige as Ben-Gurion, who had been Prime Minister in 1960, that he could afford to ignore the threats coming from the Arabs as Ben-Gurion had done. Also, the Israeli military were perfectly sure that Israel was more than a match for the Arab forces all around it, and they did not wish the newly born joint military command between Jordan, Egypt and Syria to blossom into a serious and threatening reality.

Nasser's brinkmanship and threatening gestures, even if they were intended to be no more than gestures, had therefore created a situation which was running out of his control. On 5th June, 1967, when the Israelis had skilfully lulled all but the keenest observers into thinking that the crisis had passed, they struck.

Why was there no peace?

When the fighting stopped, the Israelis had occupied about 26,000 square miles of Arab land belonging to Egypt, Jordan and Syria, in clear violation of a basic principle of the United Nations Charter. Israel's official losses were reported as 778 killed, 2,586 wounded, and 21 taken prisoner (of whom five were killed by angry mobs). Israel took prisoner over 11,500 Arabs, of whom the majority were Egyptians. Of these, about 6,000 were released immediately, as the Israelis were unable to cope with all the Egyptian prisoners they overran in the Sinai desert; the remainder, especially senior officers, were kept, to exchange for Israeli prisoners-of-war. The Israelis captured 300 Arab officers, including nine generals and 10 colonels. A month later, they claimed to have ferried across the Canal another 6,000 Egyptians, whom they had rescued

Territories occupied by Israel in the 1967 war.

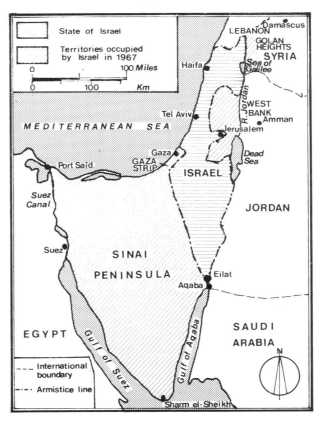

from the desert where they were struggling to find their way home without food, water, or transport. Retreating Egyptian forces from the Sinai were interned by the Egyptian authorities in special cantonments in Egypt, and some of those swimming the Canal were fired on by their own side. It is believed that this was done in order to prevent them from telling the truth about the defeat of the Egyptian Army in Sinai to the population at home, who did not learn the full extent of the disaster for a long time.

The Arab states have never given an official account of their losses, but some indication of the scale of the disaster was given in President Nasser's description of the Egyptian military situation at the time of the cease-fire: "We had no defence on the west bank of the Suez Canal . . . the road between Suez and Cairo had not a single soldier on it. The road to Cairo was open . . . paralysis afflicted our armed forces . . . . We had lost about 80% of our military equipment . . . our forces were dispersed and half bewildered . . . . We did not have aircraft to meet the enemy air force." Estimates have put total Arab losses at some 4,300 men killed, and 6,000 wounded, with another 7,500 captured or missing.

The Arabs face their defeat

After their crushing and humiliating defeat in June 1967, the member states of the Arab League convened a summit meeting to decide on a common policy in the face of their disaster. All the member states attended except Syria, which called for a "people's war" against Israel and boycotted the whole proceedings. President Nasser had resigned on 9th June, as soon as the Egyptians had stopped fighting, taking the responsibility for the defeat upon himself. Massive popular demonstrations in the streets then demanded that he remain in office, and he agreed to do so. He participated in the summit which was held in Khartoum, the capital of Sudan, from 29th August to 2nd September, 1967.

Faced with an enormous loss of territory, which they had no immediate prospect of regaining by military means, the Arab states refused to contemplate the trading of these territories in return for a peace treaty with Israel. Indeed, they regarded Israel's acquisition of its original territory in 1948/49 as illegal, and they had never recognized Israel as a state. They were not going to do so now. The Arabs did not accept that Israel should be allowed to reap "the benefits of its aggression". The conference in Khartoum became famous for its triple "no". The formal resolution stated that "there shall be no peace with Israel, no recognition of Israel, no negotiations with Israel and that the Arab nation shall take action to safeguard the right of the people of Palestine to their homeland."

In a show of solidarity with the front-line states, Egypt, Jordan and Syria, three of the Arab oil states, Saudi Arabia, Kuwait and Libya, agreed to pay them annually a total of £135 million, "until such time as all consequences of the aggression shall be eliminated".

The Israelis rejoice in their victory

In Israel, General Dayan, the Minister of Defence, spoke immediately after the war of waiting for a telephone call from King Hussein of Jordan to discuss a peace treaty. By their victory, the Israelis had conquered all the area of the former Mandate of Palestine, plus the Golan Heights taken from Syria and the Sinai Peninsula taken from Egypt. But a great wave of confidence and exultation swept over Israel and many insisted from the start that they should annex all the occupied lands, as indeed in 1949 Israel had retained all the territory it had won in the war. "Greater Israel" movements proliferated and Menachem Begin's Revisionist Party (Gahal) provided the expansionists with organized political expression – "No evacuation – even with peace" was their platform. As General Dayan admitted, "It is perhaps possible to conclude peace treaties between ourselves and our Arab neighbours, but the Arabs are asking too high a price and I pray heaven that the day never comes". He could be confident that it never would, for he knew that King Hussein was hardly likely to accept the terms he would be offered by the Israelis, if he made his telephone call. "If they don't want to talk with us . . . then we shall stay where we are, and there will be an absolutely new Israel in the Middle East," Dayan told American interviewers.

There were some in the Israeli government who hoped that the massive defeat which the Arabs had suffered would bring the Arab states to the negotiating table. However, the actions quickly taken by Israel soon demonstrated that there were certain matters about which they were not prepared to negotiate at all. The *New York Times* newspaper wrote at the end of 1967 that "Israel is deeply divided on how to go about achieving peace . . . . Even Cabinet ministers believe that the government will fall if it is forced to decide what is negotiable and what is not . . . . For the moment they have decided not to press the issue, since direct negotiations with the Arabs are not an immediate prospect . . . . The people of Israel, on the other hand, have made their decision. The overwhelming sentiment of the Israeli public favours Israel's keeping all the territory acquired during the war and working out the demographic problem as best she can. The root of this sentiment, which cuts across all party lines, is a shared conviction that a peace treaty with the Arab countries would not be worth the sacrifice of land and security . . . . [Also] the ferocity of the war . . . has not been forgotten."

On 28th June, 1967, 18 days after the end of the war, the Israeli Parliament, the Knesset, passed legislation incorporating the occupied Arab sector of Jerusalem into a reunited city under Israeli sovereignty. At the same time, the boundaries of the municipal area of Jerusalem were greatly extended, reaching to near Bethlehem in the south, and incorporating Kalandia airport (close to Ramallah) in the north. In the face of Israel's effective annexation of the Arab sector of the city, the UN General Assembly ruled that this action was invalid and called on Israel not to take any measures that would alter the status of the city. Before the resolution had been passed, Israel had already embarked on a series of structural alterations and demolitions in the Old City which aroused bitter Arab protests and were soon to change the face of Jerusalem. In spite of the international controversy that its actions provoked, the Israeli government made no secret of its determination to establish a hold on Jerusalem which would prove unbreakable.

A new wave of Palestinian refugees

Some 355,000 Palestinians fled during the fighting and after the war, from the West Bank to the East Bank of the river Jordan. Many of these people were refugees from the 1948 war, and were now uprooted for the second time in their lives. The Arabs accused Israel of deliberately expelling Palestinians from the West Bank and Gaza Strip, a charge which the Israelis denied. The UN Special Representative, in his report, stated that he had "received no specific reports indicating that persons had been physically forced to cross to the East Bank. On the other hand, there are persistent reports of acts of intimidation by Israel armed forces . . . . The truth seems to lie somewhere between an Israel statement that 'no encouragement' was given to the population to flee, and the allegation about the use of brutal force and intimidation . . . . The inevitable impact upon a frightened civilian population of hostilities as such, particularly when no measures of reassurance were taken, has clearly been a major factor in the exodus."

The Israeli government agreed to permit some refugees to

Arab refugees from the Israeli-occupied West Bank cross the blown-up Allenby Bridge to Jordan on 15 June 1967 after the war was over.

return to the West Bank, but would not have them all. They insisted that only those to whom they issued permits would be allowed to go back to their homes, and that they must return before 31st August, 1967. In spite of diplomatic wrangles, applications for repatriation had been distributed, filled out and returned to Israel by mid-August. Jordan claimed that these forms covered some 150,000 persons, while according to Israel the figure was only 100,000. Israel stated that applications for 20,658 persons were approved, whereas Jordan asserted that only 18,236 persons received permission to return. By the Israeli-imposed deadline of 31st August, only 14,056 people had actually crossed back into the West Bank.

Israeli sources blamed the low numbers returning on Jordan's inefficiency and the fact that some people evidently feared accusations of collaboration with Israel if the West Bank later returned to Jordanian rule. However, Jordan's Prime Minister, Sa'ad Jum'a, stated that Israel had deliberately restricted repatriation to a token number of people sufficient for propaganda purposes in reality, approved applications had been handed to Jordan too close to the deadline to be used, young men had been excluded, even when their families were allowed to return, thus splitting families, and furthermore, most applications of those refugees originally displaced in 1948, as well as those of persons from East Jerusalem, Bethlehem and Jericho, had been totally rejected. The Commissioner-General of UNRWA (United Nations Relief and Works Agency for Palestine Refugees in the Near East) reported to the General Assembly of the UN in October 1967 that "wherever the responsibility may lie", only a "small fraction of the total number of persons applying to return have so far been permitted to do so . . . . It is clear . . . that the hopes . . . that at least the bulk of the displaced persons would be able to return to the West Bank . . . have not been realized." The Jordanian authorities, the report continued, had done all that was humanly possible to ensure that those permitted to return "were promptly informed and given every assistance in recrossing the river".

Israel tightens its grip Israel immediately set about consolidating and reinforcing its control over the occupied territories. As early as September 1967, it began to establish Israeli settlements in the West

Historic superpower talks: President Johnson of the USA (right) with Soviet Prime Minister Kosygin during their discussions at Glassboro, New Jersey, USA on 23 June 1967, at which the Six Day War and the Middle East situation occupied most of their time.

Bank and Gaza, to encourage the colonization of these areas by Jewish settlers, and to expropriate large tracts of Arab land for cultivation and "military and security needs".

Diplomatic deadlock

Following the Khartoum summit, there was total deadlock between the Arabs and the Israelis. The Arabs refused to negotiate directly with Israel, while the Israelis, for their part, refused to consider anything but direct negotiations. Until the Arabs agreed to their terms, Israel was determined to maintain its occupation of all the territories conquered during the war. Against this background, the UN Security Council met in autumn 1967 to consider the situation. After a number of draft resolutions failed to gain approval, on 22nd November, 1967, the Security Council unanimously adopted a resolution prepared by the British delegate, Lord Caradon, which was to remain the basis for all subsequent peace initiatives.

Resolution 242 precariously bridged the gap between Arab and Israeli positions, as supported by their respective superpower allies, the Soviet Union and the United States. By condemning the acquisition of territory by war, the resolution satisfied Arab and Soviet demands for an Israeli withdrawal. Yet, because it did not specify the extent of the withdrawal, or just how much land was to be handed back, it was acceptable to the Israelis and the Americans. Subsequent arguments centred around whether the Israelis would have the right to retain parts of the Arab territories occupied during the war, in return for a definitive peace treaty.

◁ *Soviet Prime Minister Kosygin shakes hands with the UN Secretary General U Thant, as the Soviet delegation arrives in the UN General Assembly for an Emergency Session on the Six Day War on 17 June 1967. Between them is the Soviet Foreign Minister Andrei Gromyko.*

How long could "No peace, no war" last?

Israel had hoped that the impact of the crushing military defeat which it had inflicted on its Arab neighbours would bring it peace. In the euphoria which engulfed Israel in the wake of the war, the public, revelling in this demonstration of Israel's power, felt that it did not matter if the Arabs refused to make peace: Israel was secure because of its proven military superiority.

The war had left the Arabs with a crushing sense of humiliation and defeat. Rather than capitulate, they resorted to defiance (see the previous chapter) and committed themselves to the rebuilding of their armed forces in order to restore their shattered self-respect. Until such time as they might take on the Israelis in a full-scale war, they embarked on a kind of low-level warfare that became extremely costly.

After Israel's victory in 1967, the Arabs immediately started planning for the next war – their attack in October 1973 caught Israel by surprise. There were two important phases in the inter-war period: the War of Attrition, 1967-70, and a time of No War – No Peace, 1970-73.

The War of Attrition, 1967-70 – The Jordanian front

On the Jordanian front, Palestinian fedayeen made frequent incursions into the West Bank, to which Israel responded with reprisal raids of ever-increasing ferocity. In the early morning of 21st March, 1968, the Israelis launched an armoured attack on the small town of Keramah on the East Bank, where a large fedayeen unit was located. The Palestinian fedayeen and the Jordanian army unit stationed nearby put up stiff resistance. Nevertheless, the Israeli forces succeeded in occupying Keramah for a few hours and destroying the town and fedayeen camp. By evening, the Israelis had withdrawn back across the river Jordan to the Israeli-held West Bank.

The Israelis suffered heavier casualties than expected, and this led to considerable popular criticism at home. The Jordanians and Palestinian fedayeen both regarded Keramah as a victory, since they believed that they had prevented the Israelis from occupying a bridgehead on the East Bank, and forced them to retreat without achieving their objectives. The battle did much to raise the morale of the Jordanian army, and also had important consequences for the Palestinians. The fedayeen's role in the fighting increased recruitment to their organizations, and by 1970 the Palestinian guerrilla movement had grown virtually into a private army in Jordan.

The Egyptian front

The first skirmishes took place soon after the war was ended. The Egyptians immediately showed their determination to defend what remained to them and to deny the Israelis as far as possible the easy enjoyment of the fruits of their victory, on either a political or a military level.

The Egyptian city of Port Fuad, in the Sinai Peninsula at the northern end of the Suez Canal, had not been occupied by the Israelis during the war. About three weeks after the cease-fire, the Israelis made moves to try to take it and complete their conquest of the whole peninsula. They met with very stiff Egyptian resistance, and never made another attempt. In the following months, more clashes across the Canal invariably provoked spirited responses from the Egyptians.

The Suez Canal remains closed

A political clash arose when the Israelis tried to extract some advantage from the re-opening of the Suez Canal. Egypt had ordered the closure of the Canal on 6th June, 1967, "in view of the intervention of the US and the British government in the military aggression being launched by Israel". The Western economies were dependent on oil from the Gulf, most of which was normally exported through the Suez Canal. Its closure meant that tankers were forced to use the Cape route, and this greatly increased transportation costs. At the end of the war, the Canal was blocked by a number of sunken ships and other obstacles which it was calculated could be cleared in no more than a month. The Israelis demanded that they should be able to use the Canal, and profit from its use by others, or else they would refuse to agree to its re-opening. Egypt urgently wished to re-open the Canal, which had been a substantial source of much-needed revenue, but would not allow Israel to profit by sharing the royalties. Egypt announced that the presence of any Israeli vessel in the Canal would be viewed as a violation of the cease-fire. The Canal remained closed to all shipping and was not re-opened until 1975.

Egypt rearms

During 1968, the Egyptians proceeded with the rebuilding of their armed forces, advised and equipped by the USSR. Clashes with the Israelis across the Suez Canal developed into more systematic and serious low-key warfare. Massive artillery bombardments of Israeli positions along the Suez Canal by the Egyptians provoked huge retaliation by the Israelis, who shelled the Suez oil refineries and the cities of Ismailiya and Suez. The Egyptians, who were forced to evacuate some 400,000 people from the devastated Suez Canal zone, bitterly denounced the bombing of civilian targets by the Israelis. On 31st October, 1968, Israel launched a daring commando strike across the Canal, against strategic targets deep inside Egypt, hoping that this would force Egypt to redeploy the bulk of its troops away from the Canal zone.

Artillery harassment by the Egyptians continued, while the Israelis dug themselves into strongly defended positions along their side of the Canal. They established a line of fortifications which became known as the Bar Lev Line, after Lt General Haim Bar Lev, the Israeli Chief-of-Staff. On 8th March, 1969, a massive Egyptian bombardment opened the official "War of Attrition" which President Nasser announced that day. The "War" consisted of artillery duels across the Canal and commando attacks against units of the other side. Then the Israeli Air Force was brought in to raid Egyptian positions, the Israelis continuing their consistent policy of heavy retaliation to any attack. A continuous upward spiral of attack and response developed.

Israel raises the stakes   In January 1970 a major turning point was reached, when Israel decided to escalate the war in order to put more pressure on Egypt. The Israeli Air Force began a series of deep penetration raids against military and civilian targets in Egypt. President Nasser turned for further help to the USSR, which responded with more advanced equipment and more training personnel and advisers. This brought one of the superpowers close to direct involvement in the conflict.

On 8th August, 1970, a cease-fire sponsored by the US and supported by the Soviet Union ended the fighting between the Israeli and the Egyptian forces. The United States' Secretary of State, William Rogers, whose diplomatic efforts had brought about the cease-fire, had also been urging negotiations "to encourage the Arabs to accept a permanent peace based on a binding agreement, and to urge Israel to withdraw from occupied territory when her integrity is ensured". This policy, announced in December 1969, came to be known as the "Rogers Plan", which eventually brought about the cease-fire in August 1970. President Nasser had agreed to the cease-fire because the powerful Israeli bombing raids launched in response to the "War of Attrition" were extremely damaging to Egypt; he had no illusions that it was a preliminary to peace with Israel. He had come to the conclusion that as long as the Israelis had complete superiority in the air, "we are bleeding ourselves to death". In the respite offered by the cease-fire, he planned to build up an effective air defence system and eventually to send his army across the Canal to recapture the Sinai.

No War, No Peace   On 28th September, 1970, President Nasser died of a heart attack and was succeeded by the Vice-President, Anwar al-Sadat. Egypt's policy towards Israel was not altered by the change of leadership. Negotiations for a peaceful settlement on the basis of the "Rogers Plan" continued without any progress being made, and in May 1971 Mr Rogers made a new effort to get things moving, but without success.

By early 1972 President Sadat was coming to the conclusion that Israel was quite satisfied with the status quo that had existed since 1967, and with its continued occupation of the territory conquered in the Six Day War. Only pressure from one or both of the superpowers would force Israel to negotiate. Sadat decided that some action had to be taken that would make the superpowers and the United Nations focus their attention on the "No war, no peace" situation in the Middle East. Egypt's weak economy had been seriously damaged by the closure of the Suez Canal and by the tremendous burden of re-equipping and maintaining Egypt's armed forces. The Egyptian people demanded that their leadership recover the lands lost in 1967, and do something to rectify the wrong that had been done to the Palestinians. Sadat gambled that any change was better than the existing stalemate. He decided to go to war with Israel in October 1973, in order to break the deadlock and to create a new initiative for a Middle East settlement. Sadat adopted a codename for the war: "Sharara", meaning "spark" in Arabic. But the outcome and consequences of the 1973 War are outside the scope of this book.

In October 1973 the Egyptian army successfully attacked the Israeli troops stationed on the east side of the Suez Canal and broke through the Israeli's huge defensive sand embankment, seen here in the background. In front: one of the first Egyptian military rafts to reach the east bank of the Canal.

What did Israel's victory achieve?

From war to war   By its military conquests during the Six Day War, Israel changed the map of the Middle East. But Israel's victories did not bring it peace with its Arab neighbours, who were no more reconciled to its existence as a state than before. Some observers believe that the 1967 victory committed Israel to an unremitting conflict with the Arab world, and with the Palestinian people in particular.

The meaning of defeat   For the Arab states, the humiliating defeat at the hands of Israel led to much criticism of their military forces and political leaders. The defeat in the Six Day War has often been referred to as the Arabs' "Waterloo". Many sought to explain their failure in terms of the whole structure of Arab society, its outlook, mentality and the nature of the ruling regimes: "We talk of victory without acting to achieve it. . . . [Israel] defeated us while we were busy with meetings, congresses and endless talk" (*Al-Musawwar*, a Cairo weekly, 25 August 1967). The defeat was also seen to indicate the failure of ideas and ideologies borrowed from the West. It dealt a grievous blow to the secular Arab socialism advocated by Nasser.

Many Arabs believed that they had been defeated because they had turned away from their religion, Islam. A common explanation for the Israeli victory was that the Jews were truer to their faith than Arabs. The defeat by Israel played an important part in bringing about an Islamic revival in the Arab world, which has had far-reaching consequences for the Middle East today. The Islamic resurgence in the Middle East is partly a resistance to Westernization and the imitation of foreign cultures, at the expense of local traditions, and partly a response to disillusionment with imported ideologies which have failed to solve the Arab-Israeli dispute or deal with the problems of socio-economic dislocation and change.

Palestinian armed struggle   For the Palestinians, 1967 was almost as great a disaster as 1948 had been. Until 1967, some at least of the Palestinians had remained in their homeland under Arab, if not Palestinian, rule. After the Six Day War, all of historical Palestine was brought under Israeli control. However, 1967 gave the Palestinians the first real opportunity to take their future in their own hands. They became convinced that only the Palestinians themselves could recover their homeland.

The post-war period saw a new mood of militancy among Palestinians. The guerrilla movements, which had been of little significance before 1967, stepped up their armed struggle against Israel. New recruits from the refugee population flocked to join them. Fatah, led by Yasser Arafat, was by far the most important group. Although challenged by several groups with different ideas and policies, it has dominated the Palestine Liberation Organization since 1969. In that year, Arafat was elected Chairman of the Executive Committee of the Palestine Liberation Organization, a post he continues to hold.

Although the guerrillas gained considerable success, the Israelis gradually tightened their control over the occupied territories. Furthermore, Israeli retaliation raids against Palestinian bases in neighbouring Arab countries caused the governments of these countries to restrict guerrilla activities. In these circumstances, while not abandoning armed struggle, the PLO has turned increasingly to diplomatic means to achieve at least some of its objectives.

Palestinian diplomacy The Palestine National Charter calls for the total liberation of Palestine, and the PLO is committed to the idea of a single, secular, democratic state in Palestine. Nevertheless, the PLO has expressed its willingness to accept a compromise position involving the creation of a mini-state in the West Bank and Gaza. In June 1974 the Palestine National Council declared its readiness to set up "an independent national authority in any part of the Palestinian land that is liberated". In a number of statements, Arafat has indicated the PLO's willingness to accept the existence of the State of Israel in exchange for a Palestinian state in the West Bank and Gaza.

Egypt's separate peace The American-backed Camp David Accords and the subsequent peace treaty signed by President Sadat and Prime Minister Begin of Israel in 1979 were a bitter blow and a betrayal of Palestinian aspirations. Under the treaty, Egypt regained all the Sinai Peninsula, but the West Bank and Gaza remained under Israeli military rule. During the negotiations the Palestinians were not consulted, and their claim to self-determination was abandoned in favour of an autonomy plan for the West Bank and Gaza Strip. Autonomy was supposed to bring a measure of self-rule, but not independence. As

interpreted by Prime Minister Begin, "autonomy" was entirely meaningless: the Palestinians would not even control their own drinking water. Israel's interpretation of the Camp David Accords was to seize and settle as much of the occupied territories as possible.

Greater Israel

For Israel, its victory in the Six Day War brought a heavy economic burden. A large proportion of its budget is now spent on defence. The question of the future of the occupied territories has provoked intense and bitter controversy within Israel's political establishment. The Labour Party has been prepared to consider giving up some of the territory captured, while retaining military control of certain strategic areas. The Likud party, on the other hand, has regarded the occupied territories as an integral part of "Eretz Israel" (the Land of Israel) and has firmly refused to consider withdrawing from any part of them. While few Israelis would agree to granting independence to the West Bank and Gaza Strip, many are becoming disturbed by the effect that the continued occupation of these territories, with their 1½ million Palestinians, is having on Israeli society. It is an issue frequently discussed in the Hebrew press.

Since 1967, the occupied territories have become closely integrated into the Israeli economy. By 1986, some 36% of the area of the West Bank had been brought under exclusive Israeli control and some 60,500 Jewish settlers were living in 130 settlements, in clear violation of international law. Occupation and expropriation of Arab land and water resources have forced a growing number of Palestinians to travel daily into Israel in search of work. The total number of Palestinians under Israeli rule continues to grow, and it is estimated that, by the year 2010, there will be as many Palestinian Arabs as Jews in Israel and the occupied territories. This poses a serious threat to the identity of the Israeli state.

The Palestinian Uprising

After over 20 years of Israel's military rule, the pent-up frustrations of Palestinians, many of whom have been born and brought up under occupation, erupted in December 1987 into a popular uprising in the West Bank and Gaza Strip. The often brutal suppression of these demonstrations by the Israeli Army shocked world opinion, and Israel was widely condemned for its actions.

On 31st July, 1988, King Hussein of Jordan formally relinquished Jordanian claims to sovereignty over the West

◁ *Yasser Arafat, Chairman of the Palestine Liberation Organization, addressing the UN General Assembly on 13 November 1974.*

A confrontation during the Palestinian Uprising in the Israeli-occupied territiories on 12 March 1988. A young Palestinian prepares to throw stones at Israeli soldiers charging down a Ramallah street while the soldier on the left starts to fire teargas at demonstrators.

Bank, and this encouraged some Israelis to demand the territory's annexation.

Both Palestinians and Israelis continue to live with the bitter legacy of the Six Day War.

Further reading

M. Benvenisti, *The West Bank Data Base Project 1987 report*, Jerusalem Post, Jeusalem, 1987

O. Bull, *War and peace in the Middle East*, Leo Cooper, 1976

R. Churchill and W. Churchill, *The six-day war*, Heinemann, 1967

M. Dayan, *Story of my life*, Weidenfeld and Nicolson, 1976

T. Dupuy, *Elusive victory: the Arab-Israeli wars, 1947-1974*, Macdonald and Jane's, 1978

M. Heikal, *The road to Ramadan*, Collins, 1975

D. Hirst, *The gun and the olive branch: the roots of violence in the Middle East*, Faber, 1977. 2nd rev. ed., Faber, 1983

Hussein, King of Jordan, with V. Vance and P. Lauer, *My 'war' with Israel*, Owen Press, 1969

Institute of Palestine Studies, *International documents of Palestine 1967*, Beirut, 1970

Israel Defence Forces, *The six-day war*, Jerusalem, 1968.

W. Laqueur, *The road to war 1967*, Weidenfeld and Nicolson, 1968

D. McDowall, *The Palestinians, Minority Rights Group*, report no. 24 (revised ed.), London, 1987

U. Narkiss, *The liberation of Jerusalem: the battle of 1967*, Vallentine Mitchell, 1983

E. O'Ballance, *The third Arab-Israeli war*, Faber, 1972

Shiloah Centre for Middle Eastern and African Studies, *Middle East record 1967*, Israel Universities Press, 1971

J. Taylor, *Pearl Harbour II: the true story of the sneak attack by Israel upon the U.S.S. 'Liberty', June 8, 1967*, Regency Press, 1980.

Index

Page numbers in *italics* indicate illustrations.